Index

Index	Page

Index

Index	Page

Index

Index	Page

Index

Index	Page

Client

Name	
Address	
Phone	
Email	
Add. info.	

Date	Time	Service	Price	Notes

Client

Name	
Address	
Phone	
Email	
Add. info.	

Date	Time	Service	Price	Notes

Client

Name	
Address	
Phone	
Email	
Add. info.	

Date	Time	Service	Price	Notes

Client

Name	
Address	
Phone	
Email	
Add. info.	

Date	Time	Service	Price	Notes

Client

Name	
Address	
Phone	
Email	
Add. info.	

Date	Time	Service	Price	Notes

Client

Name	
Address	
Phone	
Email	
Add. info.	

Date	Time	Service	Price	Notes

Client

Name	
Address	
Phone	
Email	
Add. info.	

Date	Time	Service	Price	Notes

Client

Name	
Address	
Phone	
Email	
Add. info.	

Date	Time	Service	Price	Notes

Client

Name	
Address	
Phone	
Email	
Add. info.	

Date	Time	Service	Price	Notes

Client

Name	
Address	
Phone	
Email	
Add. info.	

Date	Time	Service	Price	Notes

Client

Name	
Address	
Phone	
Email	
Add. info.	

Date	Time	Service	Price	Notes

Client

Name	
Address	
Phone	
Email	
Add. info.	

Date	Time	Service	Price	Notes

Client

Name	
Address	
Phone	
Email	
Add. info.	

Date	Time	Service	Price	Notes

Client

Name	
Address	
Phone	
Email	
Add. info.	

Date	Time	Service	Price	Notes

Client

Name	
Address	
Phone	
Email	
Add. info.	

Date	Time	Service	Price	Notes

Client

Name	
Address	
Phone	
Email	
Add. info.	

Date	Time	Service	Price	Notes

Client

Name	
Address	
Phone	
Email	
Add. info.	

Date	Time	Service	Price	Notes

Client

Name	
Address	
Phone	
Email	
Add. info.	

Date	Time	Service	Price	Notes

Client

Name	
Address	
Phone	
Email	
Add. info.	

Date	Time	Service	Price	Notes

Client

Name	
Address	
Phone	
Email	
Add. info.	

Date	Time	Service	Price	Notes

Client

Name	
Address	
Phone	
Email	
Add. info.	

Date	Time	Service	Price	Notes

Client

Name	
Address	
Phone	
Email	
Add. info.	

Date	Time	Service	Price	Notes

Client

Name	
Address	
Phone	
Email	
Add. info.	

Date	Time	Service	Price	Notes

Client

Name	
Address	
Phone	
Email	
Add. info.	

Date	Time	Service	Price	Notes

Client

Name	
Address	
Phone	
Email	
Add. info.	

Date	Time	Service	Price	Notes

Client

Name	
Address	
Phone	
Email	
Add. info.	

Date	Time	Service	Price	Notes

Client

Name	
Address	
Phone	
Email	
Add. info.	

Date	Time	Service	Price	Notes

Client

Name	
Address	
Phone	
Email	
Add. info.	

Date	Time	Service	Price	Notes

Client

Name	
Address	
Phone	
Email	
Add. info.	

Date	Time	Service	Price	Notes

Client

Name	
Address	
Phone	
Email	
Add. info.	

Date	Time	Service	Price	Notes

Client

Name	
Address	
Phone	
Email	
Add. info.	

Date	Time	Service	Price	Notes

Client

Name	
Address	
Phone	
Email	
Add. info.	

Date	Time	Service	Price	Notes

Client

Name	
Address	
Phone	
Email	
Add. info.	

Date	Time	Service	Price	Notes

Client

Name	
Address	
Phone	
Email	
Add. info.	

Date	Time	Service	Price	Notes

Client

Name	
Address	
Phone	
Email	
Add. info.	

Date	Time	Service	Price	Notes

Client

Name	
Address	
Phone	
Email	
Add. info.	

Date	Time	Service	Price	Notes

Client

Name	
Address	
Phone	
Email	
Add. info.	

Date	Time	Service	Price	Notes

Client

Name	
Address	
Phone	
Email	
Add. info.	

Date	Time	Service	Price	Notes

Client

Name	
Address	
Phone	
Email	
Add. info.	

Date	Time	Service	Price	Notes

Client

Name	
Address	
Phone	
Email	
Add. info.	

Date	Time	Service	Price	Notes

Client

Name	
Address	
Phone	
Email	
Add. info.	

Date	Time	Service	Price	Notes

Client

Name	
Address	
Phone	
Email	
Add. info.	

Date	Time	Service	Price	Notes

Client

Name	
Address	
Phone	
Email	
Add. info.	

Date	Time	Service	Price	Notes

Client

Name	
Address	
Phone	
Email	
Add. info.	

Date	Time	Service	Price	Notes

Client

Name	
Address	
Phone	
Email	
Add. info.	

Date	Time	Service	Price	Notes

Client

Name	
Address	
Phone	
Email	
Add. info.	

Date	Time	Service	Price	Notes

Client

Name	
Address	
Phone	
Email	
Add. info.	

Date	Time	Service	Price	Notes

Client

Name	
Address	
Phone	
Email	
Add. info.	

Date	Time	Service	Price	Notes

Client

Name	
Address	
Phone	
Email	
Add. info.	

Date	Time	Service	Price	Notes

Client

Name	
Address	
Phone	
Email	
Add. info.	

Date	Time	Service	Price	Notes

Client

Name	
Address	
Phone	
Email	
Add. info.	

Date	Time	Service	Price	Notes

Client

Name	
Address	
Phone	
Email	
Add. info.	

Date	Time	Service	Price	Notes

Client

Name	
Address	
Phone	
Email	
Add. info.	

Date	Time	Service	Price	Notes

Client

Name	
Address	
Phone	
Email	
Add. info.	

Date	Time	Service	Price	Notes

Client

Name	
Address	
Phone	
Email	
Add. info.	

Date	Time	Service	Price	Notes

Client

Name	
Address	
Phone	
Email	
Add. info.	

Date	Time	Service	Price	Notes

Client

Name	
Address	
Phone	
Email	
Add. info.	

Date	Time	Service	Price	Notes

Client

Name	
Address	
Phone	
Email	
Add. info.	

Date	Time	Service	Price	Notes

Client

Name	
Address	
Phone	
Email	
Add. info.	

Date	Time	Service	Price	Notes

Client

Name	
Address	
Phone	
Email	
Add. info.	

Date	Time	Service	Price	Notes

Client

Name	
Address	
Phone	
Email	
Add. info.	

Date	Time	Service	Price	Notes

Client

Name	
Address	
Phone	
Email	
Add. info.	

Date	Time	Service	Price	Notes

Client

Name	
Address	
Phone	
Email	
Add. info.	

Date	Time	Service	Price	Notes

Client

Name	
Address	
Phone	
Email	
Add. info.	

Date	Time	Service	Price	Notes

Client

Name	
Address	
Phone	
Email	
Add. info.	

Date	Time	Service	Price	Notes

Client

Name	
Address	
Phone	
Email	
Add. info.	

Date	Time	Service	Price	Notes

Client

Name	
Address	
Phone	
Email	
Add. info.	

Date	Time	Service	Price	Notes

Client

Name	
Address	
Phone	
Email	
Add. info.	

Date	Time	Service	Price	Notes

Client

Name	
Address	
Phone	
Email	
Add. info.	

Date	Time	Service	Price	Notes

Client

Name	
Address	
Phone	
Email	
Add. info.	

Date	Time	Service	Price	Notes

Client

Name	
Address	
Phone	
Email	
Add. info.	

Date	Time	Service	Price	Notes

Client

Name	
Address	
Phone	
Email	
Add. info.	

Date	Time	Service	Price	Notes

Client

Name	
Address	
Phone	
Email	
Add. info.	

Date	Time	Service	Price	Notes

Client

Name	
Address	
Phone	
Email	
Add. info.	

Date	Time	Service	Price	Notes

Client

Name	
Address	
Phone	
Email	
Add. info.	

Date	Time	Service	Price	Notes

Client

Name	
Address	
Phone	
Email	
Add. info.	

Date	Time	Service	Price	Notes

Client

Name	
Address	
Phone	
Email	
Add. info.	

Date	Time	Service	Price	Notes

Client

Name	
Address	
Phone	
Email	
Add. info.	

Date	Time	Service	Price	Notes

Client

Name	
Address	
Phone	
Email	
Add. info.	

Date	Time	Service	Price	Notes

Client

Name	
Address	
Phone	
Email	
Add. info.	

Date	Time	Service	Price	Notes

Client

Name	
Address	
Phone	
Email	
Add. info.	

Date	Time	Service	Price	Notes

Client

Name	
Address	
Phone	
Email	
Add. info.	

Date	Time	Service	Price	Notes

Client

Name	
Address	
Phone	
Email	
Add. info.	

Date	Time	Service	Price	Notes

Client

Name	
Address	
Phone	
Email	
Add. info.	

Date	Time	Service	Price	Notes

Client

Name	
Address	
Phone	
Email	
Add. info.	

Date	Time	Service	Price	Notes

Client

Name	
Address	
Phone	
Email	
Add. info.	

Date	Time	Service	Price	Notes

Client

Name	
Address	
Phone	
Email	
Add. info.	

Date	Time	Service	Price	Notes

Client

Name	
Address	
Phone	
Email	
Add. info.	

Date	Time	Service	Price	Notes

Client

Name	
Address	
Phone	
Email	
Add. info.	

Date	Time	Service	Price	Notes

Client

Name	
Address	
Phone	
Email	
Add. info.	

Date	Time	Service	Price	Notes

Client

Name	
Address	
Phone	
Email	
Add. info.	

Date	Time	Service	Price	Notes

Client

Name	
Address	
Phone	
Email	
Add. info.	

Date	Time	Service	Price	Notes

Client

Name	
Address	
Phone	
Email	
Add. info.	

Date	Time	Service	Price	Notes

Client

Name	
Address	
Phone	
Email	
Add. info.	

Date	Time	Service	Price	Notes

Client

Name	
Address	
Phone	
Email	
Add. info.	

Date	Time	Service	Price	Notes

Client

Name	
Address	
Phone	
Email	
Add. info.	

Date	Time	Service	Price	Notes

Client

Name	
Address	
Phone	
Email	
Add. info.	

Date	Time	Service	Price	Notes

Client

Name	
Address	
Phone	
Email	
Add. info.	

Date	Time	Service	Price	Notes

Client

Name	
Address	
Phone	
Email	
Add. info.	

Date	Time	Service	Price	Notes

Client

Name	
Address	
Phone	
Email	
Add. info.	

Date	Time	Service	Price	Notes

Client

Name	
Address	
Phone	
Email	
Add. info.	

Date	Time	Service	Price	Notes

Client

Name	
Address	
Phone	
Email	
Add. info.	

Date	Time	Service	Price	Notes

Printed in Great Britain
by Amazon

41116101R00064